Home and Other Stories

SHERYL CONKELTON

ESSAY BY ANNE LAMOTT

HOME AND OTHER STORIES

PHOTOGRAPHS BY CATHERINE WAGNER

PUBLISHED FOR THE LOS ANGELES COUNTY MUSEUM OF ART

BY THE UNIVERSITY OF NEW MEXICO PRESS

Published on the occasion of the
exhibition *Home and Other Stories:
Photographs by Catherine Wagner,*
May 27 - August 8, 1993.
Organized by the Los Angeles County
Museum of Art.

LIBRARY OF CONGRESS
CATALOGING-IN-PUBLICATION DATA

Conkelton, Sheryl.
  Home and other stories: Photographs by
Catherine Wagner/Sheryl Conkelton: essay by
Anne Lamott. — 1st ed.
    p.   cm.
"Published on the occasion of the exhibition . . .
May 27–August 8, 1993, organized by the Los
Angeles County Museum of Art"—T.p. verso.
Includes bibliographical references.
  ISBN 0-8263-1455-4.
  ISBN 0-8263-1456-6 (pbk.)
  1. Photography of interiors—Exhibitions.
  2. Interior decoration–United States—
Exhibitions. 3. Wagner, Catherine—Exhibitions.
I. Wagner, Catherine. II. Los Angeles County
Museum of Art. III. Title
TR620.C66   1993
770 .4 092—dc20   92‒47043
                                   CIP

Photographs courtesy of Catherine Wagner
and Fraenkel Gallery, San Francisco, except
where noted.

Design: Catherine Mills

FOREWORD

Throughout her career, Catherine Wagner has consistently photographed the built environment. She has pictured buildings, public monuments, and classrooms. In her latest project, titled *Home and Other Stories,* Wagner turns to the home, a compelling and accessible subject, to investigate not only cultural issues but to also examine the nature of subjectivity and individual intent.

As she photographed in homes around the country, Wagner responded to the idiosyncrasy and individual expression in the domestic scenes before her camera. Special objects and carefully arranged ensembles are displayed in her images, hinting at the unseen personalities. They invite the viewer to conjure up stories about who the homeowners might be. Every home is represented differently, some by precious things, others by the evidence of interrupted activity, still others by the pictures—both photographic and painted—of themselves and their family.

Home and Other Stories provides a personal survey of contemporary American domesticity and is also an optimistic project developed out of an informed understanding of photography. It is an intellectual endeavor, the method and the structure of which compel the viewer to consider the meaning of the series as a whole. Wagner does not use straight photography as a picture of reality; instead, she emphasizes those aspects of the medium that show it to be a mode of inquiry: changing her point of view, her distance from subjects—even the subjects themselves change from triptych to triptych. Referring to important photographic models such as the work of Walker Evans or Bernd and Hilla Becher, Wagner constructs the notion of a photograph as a fragment, a possibility, an interpretation rather than an authoritative statement or factual evidence. She carefully structures her images and their sequencing to present both the individuality of her subjects and the possibility of multiple interpretations. In *Home and Other Stories* Wagner challenges the notion of a single, collective ideal, whether it be a particular kind of domesticity or the authority of photographic depiction.

The exhibition of *Home and Other Stories* provides an opportunity to consider how we define ourselves through our choice of things to live with and what role photography can play in the process of personal invention. For their generous support of this project we are indebted to Gay Block, Fraenkel Gallery, the Ralph M. Parsons Foundation, Michael and C. Jane Wilson, and Paul Yuen. I thank Sheryl Conkelton for her commitment to this program and for her fine effort in organizing this project.

MICHAEL E. SHAPIRO, DIRECTOR

ACKNOWLEDGMENTS

MUCH EFFORT goes into the production of a project like this and from the very beginning colleagues generously offered consultation and assistance. I would like to thank Lewis Baltz for introducing Catherine to me and for helping to set this project in motion. Dana Asbury of the University of New Mexico Press, who was instrumental in the realization of this book, deserves special acknowledgment for her early and enthusiastic support. I am also grateful to Catherine Mills for her innovative book design. I am appreciative, too, of Anne Lamott's imaginative essay, which provides a wonderful creative foil to my analytic prose. For important discussions about the project and their very generous and constructive advice I'd like to thank Marvin Heiferman and Joseph N. Newland. The active interest and support of Theresa Luisotti, R. Joseph and Elaine R. Monsen, John Randolph and Bruce Tomb, and Amy Richlin must also be acknowledged. Jeffrey Fraenkel and Frish Brandt of Fraenkel Gallery in San Francisco were especially helpful. I am grateful to Anne Wilkes Tucker for her early insight into Catherine Wagner's work and for her good example. For their contributions and their spirit of collaboration I am indebted to my colleagues at the museum: Elizabeth Algermissen, Victoria Blyth-Hill, Peter Brenner, Andrew Ferren, Judi Freeman, Tom Jacobson, Marlene Kristoff, Martha Drexler Lynn, Renee Montgomery, Art Owens, John Passi, Mitch Tuchman, and Lisa Vihos. Robert Sobieszek and Eve Schillo in my own department played central roles in bringing the project into being. I would like to thank former museum director Earl A. Powell III for his support, not only for this project but for the photography department program as a whole. The enthusiastic support of director Michael E. Shapiro is very much appreciated. And, finally, I thank Catherine Wagner for her wonderful art and for her good humor, her intelligence, and her friendship.

SHERYL CONKELTON

IN THE WINTER of 1989 the home I had lived in for almost ten years was sold. Urgently needing a new place to live, I began my search, eventually looking at over one hundred homes. In each, I was mesmerized by its representation of family, comfort, love, alienation, isolation, pride, privacy, and refuge, as well as recurring themes of memory. I began working on *Home and Other Stories* that winter when I asked my new neighbors, people I was meeting for the first time, if I could photograph their homes. This book is dedicated to all of those people who so willingly opened their homes for my investigation. I would like to acknowledge gratefully the National Endowment for the Arts for awarding me a Visual Artist Fellowship in 1990-91 to support the project. There are numerous people who facilitated my work in various ways: Deborah Lohrke was an incredible assistant both on the road and in the studio; her understanding, skills, and friendship made this project possible. Once again, the photographs were meticulously printed in collaboration with Simon Yuen, whose eye for detail is unmatched. A heartfelt thank-you to Shimshon Wigoder for six years of different kinds of conversation that will last a lifetime, and to Cathy Cassel for conversations now and other times too that are proving to be of great value. There is a group of people with whom I shared ideas about this project, life, and other matters of the heart: Lewis Baltz, Tom Barrow, Frish Brandt, Ann Chamberlain, Jeffrey Fraenkel, Hal Fischer, Merry Foresta, Hung Liu, Ron Nagle, Meridel Rubenstein, Sibila Savage, Leslie Smith, and Anne Wilkes Tucker. I am most grateful to Anne Lamott for her essay; her writing takes the form of a valued gift. I wish to thank Catherine Mills for her creative book design. I thank John Randolph and Bruce Tomb of the IOOA (Interim Office of Architecture), for their contributions to the installation design for the exhibition at the Los Angeles County Museum of Art. Sheryl Conkelton, the curator of this exhibition and author of this book, has been from our first meeting insightful, challenging, and intellectually stimulating. The working collaboration between artist and curator has been a joy. Finally, I thank Loretta Gargan, with whom I continue to share in the process of making a home.

CATHERINE WAGNER

SHERYL CONKELTON

Home and Other Stories and Other Stories

THE IDEA OF HOME HAS MANY RESONANCES. Home is perceived as shelter and sanctuary, a profound complex of ideas and emotions, a conceptual enterprise as well as a specific location—it is a potent expression of culture and of the individual. *Home and Other Stories,* a photographic project by Catherine Wagner, takes these precepts as its starting point. Each three-part work shows various aspects of one American home: rooms or portions of rooms and objects in ensembles that are carefully arranged for visitors or carelessly disposed in privacy. These are objects that have been chosen for their beauty, status, nostalgia, or utility in their owner's eyes; items have been selected to contribute to a sense of well-being, to make the shell of a house into a home by some person or persons unseen and unknown. Wagner's project is a display of individual aspiration on a number of levels, not only that of the unseen owners but also her own, and that of the viewers of these images who are asked to complete these works with their own stories.

This body of work is significant not only for its subject but for the treatment of that subject. Wagner's intent with this project is to show a range of domestic expressions that represent the personal and the subjective, and, perhaps most important, to demonstrate a multiplicity of points of view that suggest a generosity of spirit and a political openness. This series is not merely about Wagner's relationship to the idea and ideal of home—although it is most certainly that; it is also a portrayal of the possibility of individuality, the usefulness of seeking that individuality, and the ultimate recuperative power of individual expression. Her message is a potent one, and while the ostensible subject is easily apprehended, her method is most complicated and self-conscious. In *Home and Other Stories,* Wagner challenges many of our assumptions about photography: she addresses this project not only to the

creative spirit within the homes depicted, and within her own point of view, she also critiques photographic history in a bold attempt to display a new model for photographic storytelling. Rather than discuss the subjects of her pictures, this essay will focus on the central, critical aspects of her project and analyze the construction of the work and its place in the history of photography.

The idea of home is significant to Wagner on both personal and professional levels. Her investigation is timely; she shares her domestic subject with many American artists who currently find the topic a potent one.[1] She became interested in its visual representation when she needed suddenly to find a new place to live and began to enter people's homes in search of a house to buy. Intrigued by the households she visited and the diversity of expression, Wagner recognized that the idea of home had undergone a profound shift, much of it occuring during her own lifetime. Following World War II the materialist idea of home was an important part of the American economy and a measure of opportunity and success—the dream house became a unifying element in a newly prosperous postwar society.[2] Promoted by government programs and commercial advertising, it was perceived as a just reward for hard work. Over the course of Wagner's generation, economic circumstances have changed, placing home ownership outside the reach of many people who grew up expecting that their success would include it. The growing diversity of people and cultural ideals within most American cities also moved away from a shared model of any sort. The idea of home—as family center, as personal expression, as material display—is in the midst of a considerable transformation as pressure to recognize social and economic diversity begins to supplant the ideal of unified goals and assimilated differences.

Wagner has recognized a locus of cultural anxiety in these shifting social mores, and *Home and Other Stories* is her visual exploration of this arena.

The relationship of social expectations to individual aspirations is complicated and problematic. The construction of these homes is based on layers of memories of the past and aspirations for the future, and it is informed by myriad cultural influences: political agendas, shelter magazines, televised glimpses into the homes of the rich and famous. For the last fifteen years, many artists have explored the notion that our significant ideas and efforts come from such mediated, cultural bases. A central theme of artmaking during this time has been the primacy of the image over reality as a basis for the formation of ideas: the landscape from which our ideas and beliefs are produced is not natural but a construction based on a cultural collectivity rather than individual, authentic experience. As Paula Marincola stated in a catalogue essay for the groundbreaking exhibition *Image Scavengers* in 1982, the mass media image has become "so pervasive and so effective in imposing its conventions on the collective psyche that it somehow radically foreclosed the possibilities for authentic perception or experience."[3]

Wagner acknowledges the significance of mediated ideas, and her work is informed by previous theoretical and philosophical arguments about the impossibility of authenticity and individuality.[4] Her investigation, in fact,

incorporates a critical awareness of these ideas into a strong proposal of their exhaustion. She is motivated more by the ambiguity to be found in the balance of public and private influences than she is convinced by the argument that it is solely the social sphere that determines any expression. Wagner's purpose in *Home and Other Stories* is the display of individual intention, and she is interested in the issue of media influence only insofar as it is part of the individual's struggle to create identity. While the postwar generation of Americans may have grown up knowing Donna Reed, her happy family, and her well-appointed televised living room, the more significant issue, as Wagner has defined it, is what each individual has done with that and other media-generated ideals and relationships.

In terms of her own work and its history, *Home and Other Stories* represents a large shift in program and sensibility for Wagner. With it she moves very deliberately from the collective sphere into an individual and private realm. Her earlier photographic projects focused on larger, constructed entities in the public arena, and she worked with single, synoptic images. Her first photographs, made in the mid-1970s, considered the erection of suburban, often prefabricated, industrial structures. From these utilitarian constructs she moved to the building of the George Moscone Convention Center in San Francisco, which she traced from excavation in 1979 to finished structure in 1984; then to the Louisiana World Exposition complex in New Orleans, where she photographed its construction and use in 1984; and, finally, to the exploration of the American classroom in the mid-1980s, the still portraits of which reflect the values that shape and maintain the culture. Each of these previous series investigated the projection of certain goals and ideals through material constructions that were part of the larger social landscape, the realm of the public.

The built environment remains Wagner's stage in *Home and Other Stories,* but the object of her inquiry has shifted from the "history painting" of significant monuments built by some consensual agreement to the "still lifes" of individual, private expressions of the self in domestic settings. By investigating the profusion and diversity of responses, Wagner moves from the rhetorical to the specific. The ordered spaces displayed in her images are not composed by artists or necessarily for consumption by others. These places have been constructed to approximate someone's ideal of domestic comfort and to satisfy their own notions of who they are on a private scale. These are ordinary spaces, some very minimally outfitted, others dense and full of affect; each is informed not by an educated artistic hand but by individual memory and desire.

In her portrayal of these intimate spaces, Wagner directs attention not only to the objects and the places but to the strategies of self-recognition and aspiration that these homes represent. By picturing only the things and not the people who chose and arranged them, the personalities are not declared and the viewer can be involved in the constructing of identities, in the creation of stories about the homes and their owners. The titles of the individual works within the series reflect this intention: each title includes the names of the individuals that occupy that home. This strategy indicates the importance for Wagner of the individual and the constructive activity that creating a home represents, whether it be the luxurious spaces of Louellen, Darryl, and their children (Plate 12) or the efforts of Martha, Antonio, and their children to establish themselves in a temporary shelter (Plate 23). Wagner seeks out these telling details, avoiding the generic and the archetypal, and displays them resolutely as eccentric and peculiar events, as hopeful gestures of unique sensibility.

Wagner's focus on the expression of individuality and subjectivity is also apparent in the scope of the project. The range of homes represented is not inclusive or exhaustive but merely wide ranging; there is no definitive statement on the nature of American domesticity. Wagner entered each home with the idea that it was a place to interpret rather than a component within a scientifically devised analysis. Discarding any socially, economically, and ethnically balanced scheme as an organizing device, she allowed an element of chance to enter the project by pursuing an arbitrary means of locating homes to photograph. Her search was based on personal contacts and referrals, which allowed her a selective rather than objective expression of location, ethnicity, and economic class. Although there is a diversity among its subjects, the project is not meant to be a conclusive statement on types of expression related to these differences. Her open, relatively undefined structure resists reduction to statistical or historical conclusion.

The optimism demonstrated in *Home and Other Stories* is a consistent and characteristic element found throughout Wagner's oeuvre. Her early work

FIG.2
LEWIS BALTZ,
Park City (PC 70),
1979, gelatin silver
print, 8 x 10 inches,
Los Angeles County
Museum of Art, gift
of Betty Freeman.

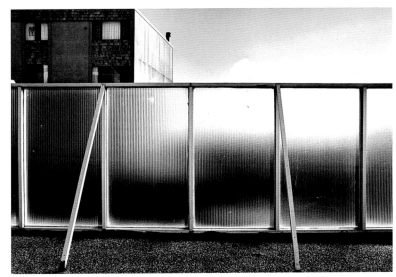

FIG.3
CATHERINE
WAGNER,
Rooftop Site II, 1978,
gelatin silver print,
11 x 14 inches

was linked to that of a group of photographers who were dubbed the "New Topographics," based on their delineative representation of the contemporary built environment.[5] Lewis Baltz, Robert Adams, and the other New Topographers focused on the banality, if not the adverse effects, of the development of suburban America, and the transparent, styleless look of their photographs functioned as an analogue to the banality and anonymity of their subjects. Wagner's images, however, presented a more optimistic view of what appears to be the same subject: she focused on the construction of order out of chaos. Her photographs of the Moscone Center in San Francisco portray the organization of rebar, cement, and pipe into a coherent public structure. Even her earliest images of various construction sites evidence this positive aspect; rather than selecting characterless elements to create a banal proscenium view, Wagner chose to picture the fundamental geometry and organizing process of the activity of erecting buildings. Her images allow a more open reading; they are less a comment upon the tedium and demoralization found by some observers in contemporary commercial architecture than they are a visual investment in the value of construction in both the physical and ideal realms.

The resemblance of Wagner's style to that of the New Topographics is drawn as much from the authority of these photographers' beautifully rendered black-and-white photographic prints as for their shared investigation of vernacular subjects. But where the New Topographics' "coherent stylistic context"[6] evokes a conceptual distance and the privileged vision of the artist, Wagner's use of the minimalist mode exploits those same stylistic characteristics for another end. She utilizes the large-format camera to yield precise description, to optimize the amount of visual information, and to present as transparent an image as possible, but her strategy is based on reducing the distance between the subject and the viewer and minimizing her own presence rather than emphasizing it. Where Baltz at times render his subjects so minimal and empty as to be almost abstract, Wagner abandoned this method very early. Her images convey information about recognizable subjects and never completely subsume them to picture-making.

It is useful in this context to compare Wagner's images with another important precedent, the photographs of Walker Evans. The photographer's physical relationship to the subject while photographing is a key element in creating the meaning of the images of both Evans and Wagner, although, of course, the specific intent of each artist is very different. Evans would often move around his subjects to make a number of photographs from different positions and from varying distances. While printing, he would select the image that best represented the subject; very often it would be the most straightforward view.[7] Evans's camera isolated subjects, even fetishized them, in absolutely balanced and tightly framed compositions. His closed forms furnish elegantly simple definitive statements; his subjects are not meant to be imagined in any other disposition.

Although in terms of clarity of style Wagner's images resemble those of Evans, their different compositional organization provides a sharp contrast. Wagner also moves around her subjects while photographing, but in selecting the best images she, on the other hand, chooses to emphasize fragmentation. By deliberately shifting her position in relationship to the subjects, she creates excerpts and tableaux rather than compositions with a consistent distance or remoteness from the subject. By using oblique views and often disregarding classical compositional balance, she is able to suggest an encounter with the subject matter rather than emphasize the formal integrity of her image-making. The images suggest an interaction of artist and subject, and a balancing of the two entities, rather than the triumph of the artist over the subject.

Wagner's stance is conceived differently, then, not only in terms of a physical position but also in terms of attitude. Her project is not about conveying some kind of essence which she has extracted from the subject by discovering the single revealing perspective. Instead, she suggests her own presence has minimal authority and strikes down the ironic distance that is so apparent in the works of Evans. Further, in *Home and Other Stories,* the viewer becomes involved in each triptych work in a cinematic way, moving through a sequence of images as well as shifting between different points of view, and relating the various elements not merely to the artist but to each other and to the viewer's space. This shifting distances the viewer from a consistent and authoritarian viewpoint and discourages the seeking of a single correct interpretation.

In essence, *Home and Other Stories* deconstructs the traditional documentary position in which the stance and attitude of the artist is readily apparent. Wagner's images confound reductivist readings. Each work is complicated by its lack of specific position within the entire *Home and Other Stories.* Although contained within the series, the relationship of each triptych to the whole is deliberately left unspecified. The viewer cannot construct narratives based on a linear structure that includes the entire set of images but may make readings of individual pieces. The spareness of the home of Christine T. (Plate 14) with its plain cardboard boxes and mostly empty refrigerator shelves conveys the sense of a spartan existence. The impending celebration implied by the birthday cake and party decorations in the rooms of James, Karyl Ann, Patrick, Annelies, Allison, and Robert G. (Plate 1) reveals a sense of potential and whimsy that is carried further by the dollhouse in the last image of the triptych. Wagner does not present any clues that would allow an easy assignation of relative status or evaluation for these readings; they may be discovered by a viewer so inclined or they can be ignored in favor of other readings. While the images themselves are very controlled, they are actually quite spare in their direction of meaning. The success of the interpretation is not based on the recognition of any particular ideas; the focus of the project is placed upon the invention of the viewer's own scheme.

The consistent look of the images and Wagner's use of a fixed format into which to insert these differently composed images would seem to be at odds

with her agenda. At first glance, each triptych closely resembles the others—each consists of three images, each is configured in the same horizontal arrangement, and all the images are the same size. The confining of these widely varying images into a seemingly homogenizing format is a strategy that alludes to the idea of typology, the analysis and classification of subjects based on types. Wagner's presentation of her images within the construct of a typology is a complex signal. Theoretically, by presenting images in a consistent manner, the similarities, gestures, and subtle differences of each articulate a relationship to a class or type. It is a means of emphasizing the characteristics held in common to define an authoritarian model or refer to an ideal type. Wagner uses a visual form that alludes to typology to introduce the notion of an ideal, then denies it in the individual images. She creates a problem for the viewer that cannot be solved; *Home and Other Stories* becomes a paradox.

Bernd and Hilla Becher's photographic typologies provide a key to the structure of *Home and Other Stories.* The regularized, multipart format and the investigation of a set of locations related by purpose is a strategy Wagner appropriated from the Becher's work to utilize in the structure of her own project.[8] By mimicking their construct, Wagner is able to signal her awareness of these earlier conventions and their meanings. But beyond the appear-

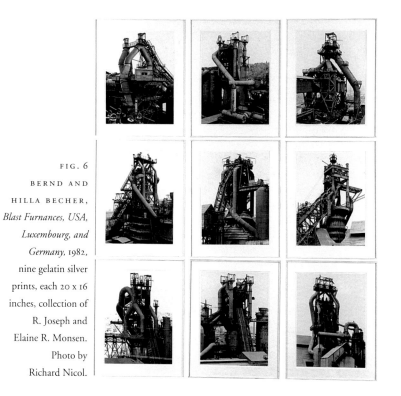

FIG. 6
BERND AND
HILLA BECHER,
*Blast Furnaces, USA,
Luxembourg, and
Germany,* 1982,
nine gelatin silver
prints, each 20 x 16
inches, collection of
R. Joseph and
Elaine R. Monsen.
Photo by
Richard Nicol.

ance—the simple sameness of format—Wagner diverges from their strategy, treating each of her subjects in an obviously different fashion. Where the Bechers utilize a grid to establish close relationships among the images, Wagner treats each triptych as a separate and discrete work, related to the others less strictly. Where the Bechers maintain an equal distance and perspective on each of their subjects, structuring their images as metrical units—flat, frontal enumerations of decontextualized form—Wagner's triptychs present very diverse views of her subjects. Where the Bechers feature the same type of building in each image, the subjects of Wagner's triptychs vary wildly in terms of the objects represented.

For example, while individual objects are isolated and given a discrete space in the home of Val N. (Plate 21), it is the ensemble of objects and their relationship to the idealized images hung on the kitchen wall that are important in Sarah F.'s home (Plate 11). Wagner recognizes these idiosyncrasies and displays them in her pictures. There is no consistent point of view or discrete subject common to all or even a majority of the homes in her triptychs; there is no constant of dining room or kitchen counter or bedroom clock, no invariable distance from her subject, no uniformity of treatment. Where the

Bechers articulate their subjects' subtle differences within a construct of strict similitude, Wagner insists on difference on both the visual and conceptual levels and displays it in very obvious ways.

Wagner's strategy in *Home and Other Stories* aligns most closely with the concerns of certain artists of her own generation. Less likely to focus their investigations upon the homogenizing effects of a media-inflected model than American artists, a number of German artists have invented post-Becher structures that acknowledge and incorporate the idea of typology to explore multiplicity and to promote the recognition of difference.[9] Candida Höfer and Thomas Struth are among the best known in the United States, and their strategies are interesting to compare to Wagner's project.[10]

Höfer, a former student of the Bechers, consistently photographs classes or types of public spaces in an exploration of their role as signifiers of social values. She uses a hand-held camera, which diffuses detail and renders an atmospheric image that is less rigorous in its reporting of actual features, enhancing instead the different mood of each space. Her images are uninhabited, and the places she depicts, while public, have an ambiguous use value. The accumulation of these "portraits" is as apparently random and without limits as is *Home and Other Stories*. Höfer's varied compositions are intuitive responses to each subject, very much like Wagner's individuated approach to each home.

Another student of the Bechers, Thomas Struth has consistently worked with series, each engaging a particular subject, such as urban space. The individual images within the series employ a uniform, centralized perspective in a manner reminiscent of the Bechers, but Struth's selection of subject and method of presentation emphasize the differences manifest in the subjects of his formally identical pictures. His photographs are conceived of as discrete images within large and relatively undefined series and have an implicit rather than explicit relationship to one another. In installation they impress the viewer as individual works whose subjects have their own integrity, appearing as almost unrelated portraits rather than works that are related conceptually and compose a series.

The images of Höfer, Struth, and Wagner share other strategies. Their images are peopleless and do not depict activity; they are not about the utility of the spaces and, although very clearly and precisely rendered, they are devoid of obvious content and without a specific story. Because of their investigation of a shared subject, their subdued style, and their consistent treatment, these works evoke the concept of typology but withhold a basis for creating the necessary relationships and evaluations.

Without that comparative basis, the groups of images assembled by these artists resemble archival structures. The meaning of individual images is not provided by the archive itself; instead an archive implies the equality and the availability of the images within. Its lack of explicit organizational structure proposes a range of possible uses for each image. Value is not exclusive to a particular purpose but is articulated as an image is discovered to be useful within a particular scheme or class devised by the current user—a purpose that may be exoteric to the archive itself but in any case is not measured by that relationship. The images in an archive may be regarded as a fragments of a whole rather than as members of a class; the images exist atomistically and their meanings fluctuate with each project.

Wagner not only draws upon this strategy, she amplifies it in *Home and Other Stories*. She privileges the elements she discovers in each subject over the correspondences that relate one to another. Although her triptychs portray members of the same type, each must be read on its own; no two function in exactly the same way. No system of characteristics may be devised, no hierarchies drawn. It is apparent that Wagner's purpose is not analytical. Within the broad construct of home she does not track any single domestic theme or paradigm but rather represents the results of choices—both the choices of the individuals who created each home and her own—within particular cultural circumstances. Hers is a cumulative structure, but not a conclusive one, and that open-endedness is precisely the point.

Wagner's strategy empowers the viewer to focus on the objects and arrangements pictured in each work and respond on the basis of that information rather than to an artistic and intellectual construct that measures and evaluates from the outside. The images acquire value as they are viewed and placed in a scheme of the viewer's own devising, which may or may not have to do with Wagner's intent. The viewer may imagine the inhabitants of the homes, may become conscious of Wagner's construct, may devise stories, and may even apply his or her own set of values to the homes that are depicted. This open-endedness implicitly engages the issue of subjectivity, and the

FIG. 7
CANDIDA HÖFER,
*Kurmittelhaus
Wenningstedt, Sylt*,
1979, chromogenic
development print
(original in color),
14 x 20¾ inches,
courtesy Galerie
Johnen & Schöttle,
Cologne.

viewer becomes actively involved in a process of locating and relocating a point of view.

This method is distinctly nonauthoritarian and relativistic, polemical if not political in its disregard for the authority of systems and their evaluating methods. The series unfolds, proposing a progressive evolution of meaning in which the parts sometimes illuminate other parts, and sometimes accumulate different meanings, but are always ambivalent and multivalent. The canonical and normative are not acceptable; Wagner uses her diverse, antiheroic, unhierarchical imagery to present her subjects without a predetermined interpretative base. Any attempt to compare the images methodically results in frustration and reveals Wagner's central construct: the pointlessness of evaluating individual expression in relationship to some universal model or abstraction, whether it the ideal middle-class home or a proscribed level of interpretation.

In proposing that viewers locate themselves within the possibility of looking both *at* her story and *through* it to "other stories," Wagner creates a hybrid model that insists that both depictive and depicted elements have weight. It has a functional similarity to a literary technique in which descriptive and emblematic elements are combined to suggest narrative possibilities. Wagner talks about the items and ensembles that she pictures as "specific objects with big stories that don't exclude the viewer"[11] and uses the very specificity of these myriad things to petition other narratives. Her minimal use of consistent, characterizing elements diminishes the sense of structure and language in a way that promotes the process of interpretation and the activity of each

FIG. 8
THOMAS STRUTH,
*South Lake Street
Apartments II*, 1990,
gelatin silver print,
17½ x 23½ inches,
courtesy Marian
Goodman Gallery,
New York.

observer in completing a work. The effect is somewhat comparable to the use of different voices in fiction; the reader or viewer shifts from first person to third person, from the artist's point of view to her or his own.

It is interesting to consider the focus of Wagner's effort. Her model more closely approximates the way in which photographs are experienced and utilized by the vast majority of people, who see the photographic object then disregard it to enter into its subject. She deliberately disregards theories that exist only as philosophical paradigms; hers is an empirical model rather than an epistemological one—one that admits not to the intrusion of voyeurism but to the primacy of looking. Her entire construct is focused on encouraging the viewer to look beyond complicated theoretical notions and consider the possibility of looking in order to perceive.

Wagner is interested in the effects of another parallel to literary method in her construct of *Home and Other Stories:* the clear portrayal of often dense detail to create a sense of transparency and immediacy. She cites the writer Annie Dillard as someone whose journalistic style and use of the essay form have had an influence on her.[12] The sheer profuseness of Dillard's literary detail suggests a hyperaware observation that recognizes the mutability of things and their narrative and evocative possibilities. In her essays, Dillard meditates upon simple, recognizable objects in a way that amplifies their presence rather than naming them and reducing them to mere fact; their presence is intensified to a wonder-full affect. The impact of Dillard's work

is based in part on the reader's experience of its density and on the suggestion of aspects of her subjects beyond those represented. In a similar way Wagner utilizes a digressive and discursive method to present images dense with the details of someone else's life, specifying only a random profusion and not overtly relating them to any structured, larger picture. Their significance is left to the viewer to presume or propose.

The analogies to literature are certainly apt; Wagner constantly refers to the storytelling power of these images and has herself received a number of stories in response to the works, such as "Oh, we had one of those" or "My grandmother lived in a house like that," followed by the recounting of a story or a memory of that object or house and a significant event related to it. Such inventions are obviously based on the viewer's memory and the strong urge to identify, inspired by and sifted with the information gained by the activity of looking. Many of the responses to the work have included not only the retelling of important occurrences but also the fabrication of stories to explain the elements in the images, interpretations that are, in reality, projections of the viewer's own desires, memories, and knowledge.

What *Home and Other Stories* offers is not the obvious story anticipated from a documentary photograph or even the synedoche of a journalistic image. Wagner's pictures are emphatically not transfigurations of the commonplace object into symbolic or totemic images. The object is not to duplicate the artist's process of interpretation, to analyze or somehow measure the subjects in these triptychs, but to formulate—to write—other stories from the mise-en-scène that confronts the viewer. Wagner consciously builds her series to proffer the notion of invention and interpretation at all stages, from the traces of individuality she discovers in the constructions of home to the endless and equal narratives that occur to the observers of these images. Wagner's project does not subscribe to a fixed system of representation but presents a hybrid that resists easy and formulaic interpretation—a challenge to the viewer to articulate a new model, to draw specifically on her or his own resources to invent a meaning.

In much of this discussion Wagner's objectives and parameters are presented within the context of what they are not. This is intentional and significant: what Wagner represents in this project is, most important, a negation of much of the prevailing theory that holds that originality is not possible in the face of overwhelmingly pervasive cultural influences, that artistic constructs cannot represent their subjects without significant and formative prejudice that preclude meaningful interpretation. As part of her negation strategy, Wagner deliberately references other artists' work in order to deconstruct the paradigms they represent. Her primary purpose in this project is the subtle demonstration of the inappropriateness of any system that would promote exclusionary evaluations.

But *Home and Other Stories* is not merely an intellectual exercise in negation. It is also a multivalent complex intended to celebrate constructive activity that works "towards openness and undoes categories."[13] Wagner asserts the recuperation of the active role of viewer as creator: looking becomes reading, reading becomes writing. The viewer becomes a proactive and inventive force. Wagner understands that part of the voyeuristic experience is a projection of self, that the process of reconstructing these personalities involves the viewer's striving to make these things familiar and understandable. Interpretation becomes a synthesis of personal recollection and spontaneous fiction, the "other stories" Wagner recognizes in her series title. As the philosopher Frederic Jameson has pointed out, narration is a central human activity, and the constructing of interpretation is a means of extricating ourselves from social codes, a means of individuating and becoming "complete and self-sufficient."[14] Wagner believes in the significance of the aspiration to create stories and in the optimistic project of constructing individual identity. What she offers is the renewed possibility of invention in the myriad small stories of *Home and Other Stories,* which is itself a large, complex, and ultimately moral tale.

NOTES

1. See the exhibition catalogue *Pleasures and Terrors of Domestic Comfort* by Peter Galassi (New York: Museum of Modern Art, 1991).

2. For a well-developed discussion of the changing role of the American home, see Dolores Hayden, *Redesigning the American Dream: The Future of Housing, Work, and Family Life* (New York: W.W. Norton, 1986).

3. Paula Marincola, "Stock Situations/Reasonable Facsimiles," *Image Scavengers: Photography,* exhibition catalogue (Philadelphia: Institute of Contemporary Art, 1982), 5.

4. See Jean Baudrillard, "The Precession of Simulacra," *Art and Text* 11 (September 1983):3-47; Rosalind Krauss, "The Originality of the Avant Garde: A Postmodern Repetition," *October* 18 (Fall 1981): 47-66. Both articles are reprinted in *Art After Modernism: Rethinking Representation,* edited by Brian Wallis (New York: New Museum of Contemporary Art, 1984).

5. Photographs by Robert Adams, Lewis Baltz, Bernd and Hilla Becher, Joe Deal, Frank Gohlke, Nicholas Nixon, John Schott, Stephen Shore, and Henry Wessel, Jr., were included in an exhibition presented at the George Eastman House in 1975 with the title *The New Topographics: Photographs of a Man-altered Landscape.*

6. William Jenkins, "Introduction," *The New Topographics: Photographs of a Man-altered Landscape* (Rochester, N.Y.: International Museum of Photography at George Eastman House), 5. In the catalogue essay Jenkins focused on the question of style and the decision to subdue style, and postulated "what it means to make a documentary photograph."

7. Jerry Thompson describes Evans's working method in "Walker Evans, Some Notes on His Way of Working," *Walker Evans at Work* (New York: Harper and Row, 1982), 10.

8. Artist in interview with the author, San Francisco, December 10, 1991.

9. This issue has been commented on by Jean-François Chevrier in his essay "Shadow and Light," *A Dialogue About Recent American and European Photography,* exhibition catalogue (Los Angeles: Museum of Contemporary Art, 1991), 17.

10. Both artists have shown their work in one-person exhibitions in the United States, and both were included in a traveling exhibition organized by the Newport Harbor Art Museum, Newport Beach, California, in 1991, *Typologies: Nine Contemporary Photographers.*

11. Artist in interview with the author, San Francisco, December 10, 1991.

12. Artist in interview with the author, San Francisco, December 12, 1991.

13. Mary Ann Caws, *The Art of Interference: Stressed Readings in Verbal and Visual Texts* (Princeton: Princeton University Press, 1989), 5. See also the first chapter on the value of disruption.

14. Frederic Jameson, *The Political Unconscious: Narrative as a Socially Symbolic Act* (Ithaca, N.Y.: Cornell University Press, 1981), 10.

ANNE LAMOTT

Another Story

YOU WONDER, what would Catherine Wagner photograph in my home? Studying the photos in *Home and Other Stories,* these interiors, these surfaces, reveal so much about who we really are, what we love, how we live, what we yearn for—and the gulf between that and what *is.* In the most mundane objects and settings—empty picture frames, two lightbulbs side by side on a rough wood table, a birthday cake in the shape of a bunny rabbit, one of those rigid handbags you could never use for anything except maybe a weapon—we see the mixture of humor and irony and love and compassion and loss and sadness that makes up our lives. We see, over and over again, the quality—the miracle—of self-forgiveness. And we see, perhaps more than anything else, our attempts to prove that we really do exist, in time and space: certainly our belongings, our knick-knacks, our clutter, our lists, our valuables and photographs and memories, prove that, don't they? I was reminded of Rilke's lines:

> *And if the earth has forgotten you,*
> *Say to the still earth: I am flowing.*
> *Say to the rushing waters, I am.*

That is what these pictures say to me: I am. We are.

So what would she photograph in our houses? What scenes and images would make up our triptychs? How would Wagner's sensibility and choices reveal our isolation and our connectedness? How would it reveal that even as the world tries to squash our individuality and our sense of discovery and wonderment, it all somehow manages to burst out the sides anyway?

I took a little journey through my rooms. I believe that Wagner sees the house as a stage, or a set, and she sees our stuff—the things we own and the way we arrange them—with a good measure of compassion and respect, as well as enormous curiosity. Viewing her work, you don't laugh at how ridiculous we are to care about our things. You feel instead moved by how we try to find meaning and beauty and connectedness; and how other times we just try to hang on.

And in the light of Wagner's vision I saw one thing I felt sure would capture her eye—a big raggedy potted plant in the corner of my living room, with half its fronds brown and withered, half green and alive. But what is the story here? For Wagner's photos tell a story; and I will tell you the story of the plant, because it applies: I'm not a big indoor plant afficionado—I like things that grow outside, and I like cut flowers, but I can't keep indoor plants alive. I'm a one-woman Bolivian death squad. My friends try to save my plants by watering them whenever possible, so the plants only half die; against all odds they continue to live. This one potted plant is the only one in my house. It's a disgrace. It's like Howard Hughes in his last days. But the thing is, with never enough love or water, and inadequate sunlight, it stays alive; in some funny way, it thrives. And I think that this is the story you see in these triptychs. People alone and in families, surviving, sometimes even thriving, against all odds.

The photos are dramatic, sometimes stark, always layered, like a meal where you taste one batch of flavors immediately, but then other, subtler, stranger flavors rise through the center of the food, bursting up to the top. The images here are so strong and clear that they enable you to step back for a moment, but then because of their oddness, their quirkiness, they suck you back in. They work on you as, at the same time, they require that you work at staying with them long enough for parts of the puzzle to be provided, and mysteries to be revealed. Look, for instance, at the birthday scene, in *James, Karyl Ann, Patrick, Annelies, Allison,, and Robert G.* (Plate 1).

Now, each person brings his or her own references to the viewing of these photographs, but my impression is that this first photo is what passes for festiveness, a party waiting to happen—the disembodied heads of the balloons, the highchair as a kind of throne. Then we see the bunny rabbit cake in the second shot, and it's kind of terrifying, as if it's from the Charles Addams bakery, so incredibly overdone and menacing, with the long sharp licorice claws, the bow like a garrote. In the third picture we can see the world at ground level, because that is what's available when you're little. On top is the huge dollhouse that your parents think you should play with. But look closer, at the vacancy of the windows, just like in the windows of the houses in the neighborhood (and maybe in the eyes of the neighbors). Then look in the top left window with the polka-dotted curtains, at the little stuffed animal trying to escape. But underneath, stashed away, are things you might love if you're small—the Breyer horse, the nearly translucent high heel, and then on the dresser, where you can't get to them, the glass swans, the tender lamp. And so as I said, at first the scene seems sort of scary and empty, as if someone was trying too hard. But the more I looked at it—in fact, the more I looked at all these pictures—the more I thought of those last pages of *Franny and Zooey.* Franny, having some sort of terrible nervous breakdown as she struggles to find anything sacred or holy in the world, has been lying on her mother's couch, day after day, saying the Jesus Prayer, starving herself, until finally Zooey, on the phone upstairs, begs her to drink the chicken soup their mother has made, crying out to her that it is *consecrated* soup, because their mother made it with love, out of the deepest possible place of love, and of wanting to help. And that that love makes it holy. This quality is partly responsible for the sense of light that you notice in so many of these pictures.

I wandered through the rooms of my house, scanning: I believe that Wagner would see stories or images in my house that are so unconsciously a part of me that I wouldn't particularly notice them. Even so, on a wall in my living room that is covered with photographs, I saw what might be the second shot of my triptych. My two-year-old son sitting in his sailor suit on our front steps, a picture of my father at the age my son is now, a picture of my son a year ago, dressed to the nines, peering into a hamper of dirty clothes with such glee that it might be a toy chest, my older brother and me as very small children, dressed in brand new pajamas, both of us with very short hair, almost crew cuts. We are smiling; I think Ms. Wagner might photograph this wall, because the snapshots are such an eloquent statement of how my family has tried to comfort itself, and how sometimes it actually worked. That's what homes are all about; that's what the pictures in this collection you are holding are all about. Comfort; continuity; in these photos, and on our walls, we see some shining moments, when against all odds, everything was okay for a while, and other moments when things felt bleak and joyless. It is the mix that's so profound. Studying Wagner's work, I kept hearing a stanza of an old song by John Prine: "Photographs show the laughs, recorded in between the bad times, happy sailors dancing on a sinking ship." And I thought of it especially when I studied the triptych *Johnnie M.* (Plate 24).

These are beautiful faces, smiling, but sometimes they convey the sense of tragedy, animal tragedy, of baboons baring their teeth; you have the sense of rictus, big smiles where the eyes aren't smiling. Look at how guarded the faces in the first photo are, all except the baby's relatively innocent face, and the guardedness of children in finery who don't feel fine at all. Look at the interlacing of hands; at our entanglements, at the ties that bind. And then look at the woman in the next photo, surely the mother grown older, beautiful, elegant, frozen, but courageous—look at the bravery in the little scarf wrapped at the waist. My first impression was that she was in trouble, that there was something wrong, and as it turned out, she was quite ill with cancer, this former femme fatale. The photographs in the third picture were the decoration on her son's wall, in the room of the now-grown baby in the first picture, the collage of photographs glued or taped to a mirror, of siblings and parents and girlfriend and self. What a bold statement of definition this collage is, of what we value, and what we need. (Sometimes our props serve to comfort and define us—a skateboard, a fancy dress, a stuffed fish, Ronald Reagan.) What contradictions in the collage—in one direction joy and celebration, and then all of sudden the mood changes—one's eye is caught by the little girl who might be retarded, and then by the beautiful, vital young woman, and then by the dumb soft-porn touches, and then around to joy again, the older child playing with the younger.

Where does this all leave us? Clearly Wagner does not intend us to walk away from these pictures with a nice complacent sense of the subjects, of families, of ourselves, something you could tie up with a nice red bow and feel comfortable about. These pictures, for all their compassion and solidarity, are disturbing, and sad—they're about the human condition, and the human condition is so often a sad one. But the primary thing I was left with was a heightened awareness of the many ways in which our homes serve as existence checks. In this surreal postmodern world that races by, pummelling us with images and information, our things, our photos, our pasts, our choices say, I exist. I am.

There's a desk in the triptych *Ron S. and Peter A.* (Plate 6) that bears an uncanny resemblance to my own, which is to say, cluttered and cramped, yet full of so many attempts at making my life more ordered, more spacious. The list, for instance; ah! I thought, here's another person who hopes life will work out more like lists than the hodgepodge fly-by-night operation it so often turns out to be. If, as Anthony Burgess wrote, time is nature's way of keeping everything from happening at once, why does time so defeat us? Why, for instance, does there never seem to be enough of it? And yet why does it so often loom emptily ahead of us, waiting to be filled like a voracious animal? The list on this desk seems simultaneously to be about hope and despair; we all know that by the time we get to all the errands and calls on the list, it's time to make another, and we're already behind. And there's the bundle of pencils, all these pesky pencils that have to be corralled, or else they'd fly off in all directions, as if in the pressureless atmosphere of a spaceship—and then where would you be when it is time to make another list?

Then look at the idealized fantasy world of the lithograph in the middle photo, its cool, sleek, urbane lines. Is this a picture that the occupant of this apartment would like to step into? Also the two great potted plants, thriving, unlike my own. Look at the one on the right, and before going any further, look at all the stuff underneath it, at what the camera sees that the eye goes right over—the detritus, the dandruff of our lives. But we raise our eyes to the plant. It's huge and fierce, like a Stephen King fern. It looks like it could definitely take over. As it fills the space in a wild and definite way, it's a comfort; most of the things in our houses are there to comfort us, aren't they? And to remind us that we are loved and connected, or at least trying.

In my bedroom I found the third photo Ms. Wagner might shoot, the sunlight falling on my bedside table, cluttered with books and toy trucks and a glass of water and some photos, all illuminated by the dim light from a small, crummy but brave little reading lamp. There are so many kinds of light in Wagner's pictures, shot very matter-of-factly, without playing up the drama. They feel true to the light that was really there. Some are shot in sunlit rooms, others at dusk; there are candles and lamps everywhere. Often we see the true lights of the house, the children, in wary and joyless portraits above or between these lamps—look, for instance at the home of Ann and Robert W. All this light, but also (look in the first photograph) all these cords, anchoring our things, throwing lights on in the darkness, helping us communicate with the world outside. Look at the television set sitting primly on the table like a guest (and the furniture digging its feet into the rug as if it might possibly be expecting trouble). One has the sense here of being backstage, of seeing the seams, of glimpsing the workings behind the set during the play, by accident. It all feels so beautifully poignant, and intimate, and weird—notice the cords of the lamp and the television set connecting the two rooms, a reminder of how, electrically and metaphorically, there are rarely outlets where and when you need them.

(I thought more than once how crazily, hilariously loud this project would be if somehow everything in these pictures came to life—the TVs and radios blared, and the portraits on the walls spoke and sang and the phones rang and the air conditioners hummed and rattled. . . .)

One has the sense of real intimacy in these pictures; they're almost voyeuristic. Again and again we see who we are in our secret interior places, see the diversity and sameness that attend our lives. For instance, as I wandered room to room in my house, looking at all the little shrines of my family and my past and my feeling for God, at the perhaps surprising numbers of vaguely tacky religious icons, I kept thinking of the home of Bert S. (Plate 4): the two kitschy, sacramental Jesuses above the smudged lightswitch, and the darkness beyond. The illusion of perfection in the living room. This is a room, like so many of the rooms in *Home and Other Stories,* that is about the deep guiding pride we take in our homes and in what we have made of our lives, and our sometimes obsessive interest in how other people see us. It too is idealized: it looks like maybe no one has ever sat in here, on the pristine antique couch; the symmetry of the gilded picture frames, and the mirror-image lamps on the tables—the whole thing is like a temple of symmetry.

FIG. 9
CATHERINE
WAGNER,
Ann and Robert W.,
Terra Linda, Ca., 1991,
gelatin silver print,
20 x 56 inches.

But the piece of the puzzle that belies it all is the crack, and the attempt at patching it, and all the poignancy contained therein. And then there's the sense of another kind of shrine in the third photograph, the clunky air-conditioner that is transformed by becoming a part of Wagner's art; and the rather joyless processed painting that still somehow speaks of hope and positivism, that takes us to a place we don't live anymore. There's the dark door and light door side by side in the photograph of the house, the plaque below and the button so oddly affixed, and one senses, as in so many of these homes, the intense, shy pride of the owner.

I guessed that this was the home of old, religious people, but what I didn't know was that Bert had inherited it from his grandparents, and out of respect for them had left it exactly as it was when they were alive. So now the pictures of these rooms feel beautiful and tragic, at once a portrait of his grandparents and also, of course, because of his love and reverence, a portrait of an oddly caring man in the postmodern world. It's about the spirit of perseverance, and continuity; it's about survival, and going on, and clinging, it is (like so many of these other pictures) about somehow surviving losses and loneliness that otherwise seem simply unsurvivable.

The beauty of these images is that you don't have to wrestle them into symbolic meaning. They are such clear pictures of the hope and despair that live in our houses, and the faith, and the wearing away of time. But left to our own devices, we gloss over the surfaces of our everyday lives, because there's so much to take in these days. These pictures make us stop for a moment, grow quiet, and go inside: they are meditations.

There are the quiet scenes—the stillness of the photos in *Pat M.* (Plate 13), with the basket full of air and light and the potatoes beginning to sprout. Maybe she was going to cook them for herself but did not get around to to it, yet another of the many things we mean to do that we never get around to. And the quietly ambiguous portrait of the woman in the next picture, and the hard pointed shape of the kitschy little statue, and the wonderful wrinkly lace, a visual trill beneath it all. (It looks like it might want to fly, but is stuck.) And then the beauty and poignancy of the two lightbulbs lying side by side—like a mother horse and her foal—on the rough wood, near the book that is waiting to be read. It's very lovely and lonely, like so many of the homes here, and not entirely comfortable.

And then there are the loud noisy portraits, like the wild clutter of *William F.* (Plate 26) that I found so oddly reassuring, not because my house is not quite so out of control, but because clutter shows us that life is being lived, piles on top of piles. You ask, what erupted? Is someone leaving or arriving? There's the feeling of movement and occupation that we didn't sense in Bert's house, a wonderful childishness about the clutter, a naughtiness. There are lots of eccentric juxtapositions—the giant slug at the end of the bed which meets Shiva nose to nose; the deflated hot water bottle on the floor sleeping in its little house. All the images of Oriental tranquility—the Buddhas, the bonsai, side by side with that cockamamie black velvet toreador painting. Clutter is such a fertile field—it means you can still fix things, still get a grip —whereas tidiness might suggest that this is as good as it's going to get; one thinks of held breath. Look, in the third photo, at all the things that seem to have escaped from the confines of the closet, a cornucopia gone crazy, spilling out more stuff than you could ever use or want—the silly striped pants, the stiff handbag that looks like a mailbox, the big lunky animal that must have seemed at one time like the best possible thing to own—junk that began as valuables, where you could almost not believe your great good fortune in owning such fabulous things. And then between the pandemonium of these bedrooms are the collector's items outside the kitchen, more scenes and statues of Oriental tranquility, and the four circles in a vertical line, a thermostat and three frames, one of which is empty: what was left out? And the two big pictures, of a man and a woman—who do you think they are?

Well, I don't know, but they are not about this time, our time; and yet, like the painting of the aged farmer in the home of Bert S., they are not about nostalgia. They are about memory. They give us layers of information and clues about time, past and present, about who we are as a people. They are, as Ms. Wagner has commented somewhere, future ruins.

So in answer to the original question, of what would she photograph in our homes: she would indirectly photograph you, she would photograph me, in kind, eclectic, wide-open glances and narrowly focused shots. She would photograph our rooms, and our things, our shrines and quirks and passions and sorrow, our pasts and hopes and our alienation, our attempts to prove that we exist and are more or less okay, our messes, and choices, all the marks and signs of human endeavor. She would photograph our fans and clocks and calendars, shelves and closets, and toys and clothes, and all the ways we keep things lit, our lights and windows and lamps and candlesticks; and all the ways that the human spirit still functions in these often spirit-deadening times, and how even though stifled, the tendrils still reach for the light.

PLATES

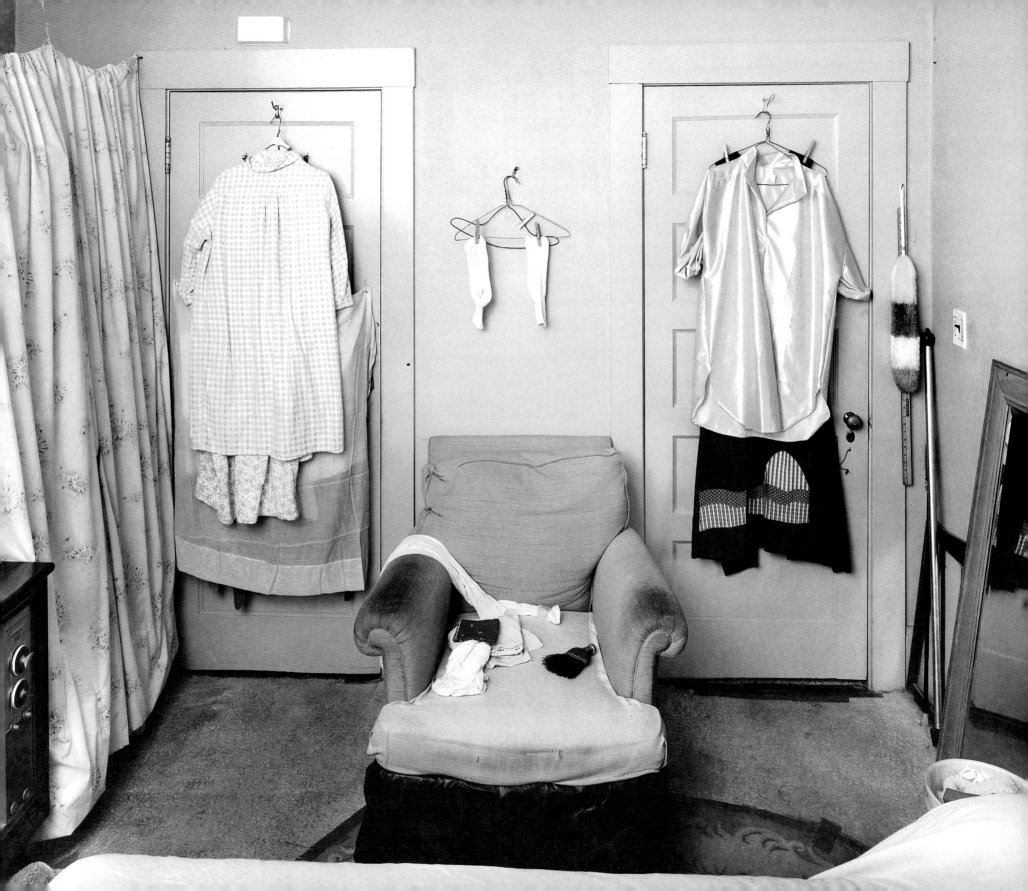

3. ERNA K., BROOKLINE, MA., 1991

4. BERT S., HOUSTON, TX., 1991

6. RON S. AND PETER A., SAN FRANCISCO, CA., 1989

7. IRENE, PETER, AND JOSH P., BROOKLINE, MA., 1991

8. ALEXANDRA M., HOUSTON, TX., 1991

9. HELEN, ROBERT, CLARE, AND CHLOE R., NEWTON, MA., 1991

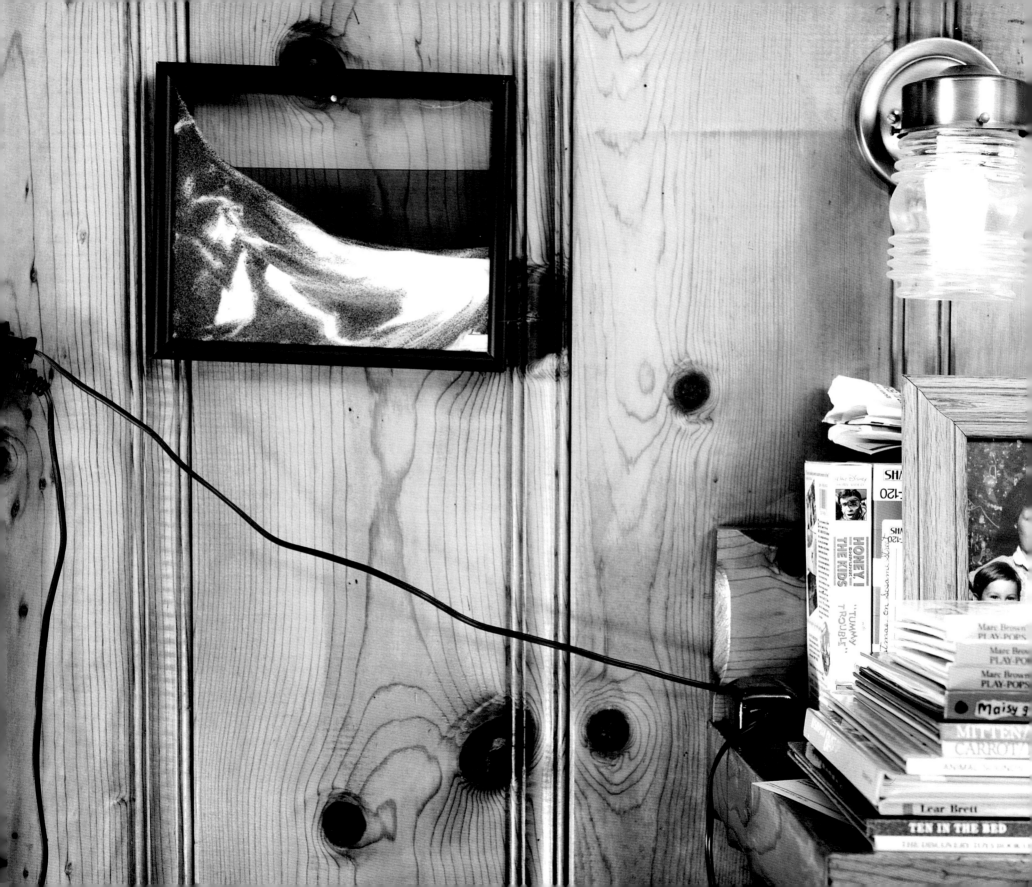

11. SARAH F., KANSAS CITY, MO., 1991

12. LOUELLEN, DARRYL, ALLISON, DARRYL, JR.,
BRANDON, AND RYAN B., NEW ORLEANS, LA., 1991

13. PAT M., OAKLAND, CA., 1991

SANTO NIÑITO PERDIDO DEL RANCHO DEL TLACUACHE. PENJAMO, GTO.

16. MARILYN AND BILL M., SAN LORENZO, CA., 1990

17. MIMI AND MEL K., BROOKLINE, MA., 1991

18. MAGGIE N., NEW ORLEANS, LA., 1991

20. DAVID W. AND ANNETTA F., RICHMOND, CA., 1990

21. VAL N., SAN BRUNO, CA., 1992

22. DIANE AND DAVID G., PIEDMONT, CA., 1990

23. MARTHA, ANTONIO, ANTONIO, JR.,
AND LUIS P., PITTSBURG, CA., 1992

24. JOHNNIE M., SAN FRANCISCO, CA., 1989

25. TOM AND PAT B., NEW ORLEANS, LA., 1991

26. WILLIAM F., KANSAS CITY, MO., 1991

27. ANNE T. AND JOE W., HOUSTON, TX., 1991

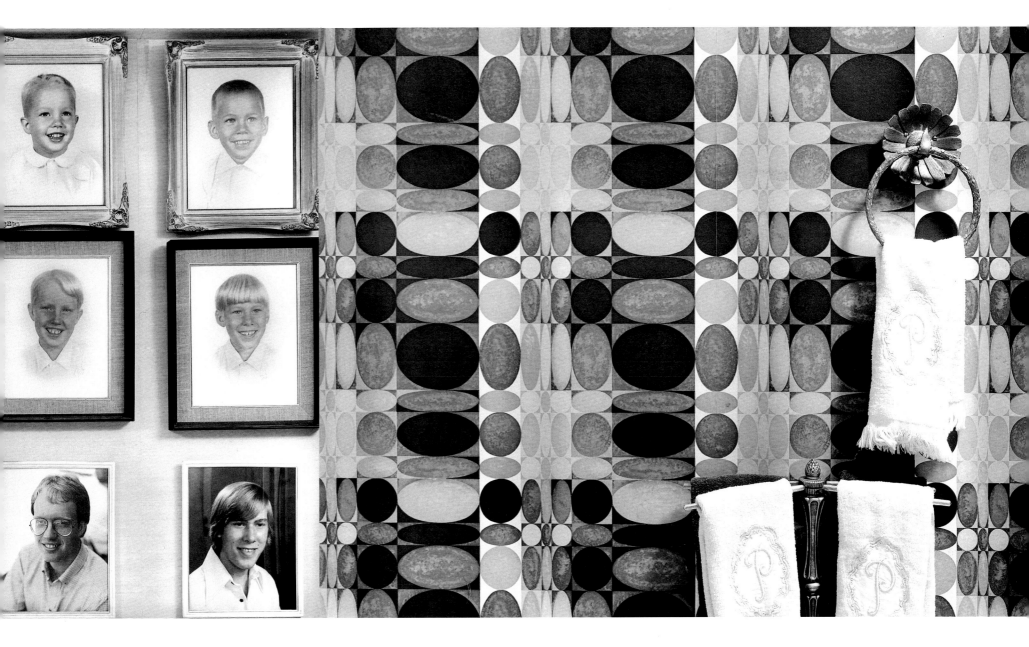

28. MONICA AND JACK P., MILL VALLEY, CA., 1990

BIOGRAPHY AND SELECTED BIBLIOGRAPHY

CATHERINE WAGNER was born in San Francisco, California, in 1953. She received her Bachelor of Arts (1975) and her Master of Arts (1977) from San Francisco State University. She is currently associate professor of art at Mills College in Oakland, California.

SELECTED AWARDS

1981
National Endowment for the Arts, Visual Artist Fellowship in Photography

1983
Mellon Foundation Grant, Mills College

1984
Ferguson Grant, The Friends of Photography

1987
John Simon Guggenheim Memorial Foundation Fellowship

1990-91
National Endowment for the Arts, Visual Artist Fellowship in Photography

SELECTED EXHIBITIONS

1977
"Cityscapes," Downtown Center Invitational Group Show, M.H. de Young Museum, San Francisco

San Francisco Art Institute, Atholl McBean Gallery (four-person exhibition)

1978
Equivalents Gallery, Seattle (two-person exhibition with Walker Evans)

Simon Lowinsky Gallery, San Francisco (one-person exhibition)

"Contemporary California Photography," Camerawork Gallery, San Francisco (catalogue)

1981
"Large Spaces in Small Places: A Survey of Western Landscape Photography, 1850-1980," Crocker Art Museum, Sacramento (catalogue)

Orange Coast College, Costa Mesa, California (one-person exhibition)

University of California at Santa Cruz (two-person exhibition with Gail Skoff)

1982
"Slices of Time: California Landscape 1860-1880, 1960-1980," The Oakland Museum, Oakland, California (catalogue)

Simon Lowinsky Gallery, San Francisco (one-person exhibition)

Equivalents Gallery, Seattle (one-person exhibition)

1983
"Facets of the Collection from the California Sharp School," San Francisco Museum of Modern Art, San Francisco

New Image Gallery, James Madison University, Harrisonburg, Virginia (one-person exhibition)

1984
"La Photographie creative," Bibliothèque Nationale, Paris, France

1985
The Oakland Museum, Oakes Gallery, Oakland, California (one-person exhibition with illustrated brochure)

"20 x 24 Polaroid Exhibition," Friends of Photography, Carmel, California

"Photography from the Permanent Collection," National Museum of American Art, Smithsonian Institution, Washington, D.C.

1986
"Bay Area Biennial," Newport Harbor Art Museum, Newport Beach, California (catalogue)

"New American Photography," Min Gallery, Tokyo, Japan (catalogue)

1987
"New American Photography," Fogg Art Museum, Harvard University, Cambridge, Massachusetts

"Catherine Wagner, 1976-86," Min Gallery, Tokyo, Japan (one-person exhibition with catalogue)

1988
"Catherine Wagner: Photographs from the American Classroom Project and the George Moscone Site," Museum of Contemporary Photography, Columbia College, Chicago (one-person exhibition)

"Changing Places: Photographs by Catherine Wagner," Farish School of Architecture, Rice University, Houston (one-person exhibition with catalogue)

"American Classroom: The Photographs of Catherine Wagner," Museum of Fine Arts, Houston (one-person exhibition with catalogue)

"Cross Currents/Cross Country," Camerawork Gallery, San Francisco and Photographic Resource Center, Boston (catalogue)

1989
"American Classroom: The Photographs of Catherine Wagner," Friends of Photography, Ansel Adams Center, San Francisco (one-person exhibition)

"Photographs 1978-1988," Fraenkel Gallery, San Francisco (one-person exhibition)

"Picturing California," The Oakland Museum, Oakland, California (catalogue)

"Theme and Variations: The Photographic Still Life," San Francisco Museum of Modern Art, San Francisco

1990
"Natural History Recreated," Center for Photography at Woodstock, Woodstock, New York

"Perspectives on Place: Attitudes Toward the Built Environment," San Diego State University, San Diego, California

"American Classroom: The Photographs of Catherine Wagner," Laurence Miller Gallery, New York (one-person exhibition)

1991
"Site Work: Architecture in Photography since Early Modernism," Photographers' Gallery, London (catalogue)

"Silent Interiors," Security Pacific Gallery, Seattle
(catalogue)

"Catherine Wagner: Selections," Turner/Krull
Gallery, Los Angeles (one-person exhibition)

"American Classroom," Cuesta College Art Gallery,
San Luis Obispo, California, (one-person exhibition)

"California Cityscapes," San Diego Museum of Art,
San Diego, California (catalogue)

1992

"To Collect the Art of Women: The Jane Reese
Williams Collection of Photography," Museum of
New Mexico, Santa Fe, New Mexico (catalogue)

SELECTED COLLECTIONS

Bibliothèque Nationale de Paris, Paris, France

Center for Creative Photography,
University of Arizona, Tucson, Arizona

Chase Manhattan Bank, New York, New York

Delaware Art Museum, Wilmington, Delaware

First National Bank of Chicago, Chicago, Illinois

Grunwald Center for the Graphic Arts, University of
California, Los Angeles

International Center of Photography, New York,
New York

J. B. Speed Art Museum, Louisville, Kentucky

Los Angeles County Museum of Art,
Los Angeles, California

The Metropolitan Museum of Art, New York,

Minneapolis Institute of the Arts,
Minneapolis, Minnesota

Museum of Fine Arts, Houston, Texas

National Museum of American Art, Smithsonian
Institution, Washington, D.C.

The Oakland Museum, Oakland, California

Polaroid Collection, Cambridge, Massachusetts

Rhode Island School of Design,
Providence, Rhode Island

San Francisco Art Commission Archives,
San Francisco, California

San Francisco Museum of Modern Art,
San Francisco, California

Santa Barbara Museum of Art,
Santa Barbara, California

Security Pacific Bank, Seattle, Washington

Tokyo Institute of Polytechnics, Tokyo, Japan

MONOGRAPHS

Catherine Wagner, 1976-1986. Tokyo: Min Gallery,
1987.

Changing Places: Photographs by Catherine Wagner.
Houston: Farish Gallery, Rice University, 1990.

Tucker, Anne Wilkes. *American Classroom, The
Photographs of Catherine Wagner.* Houston:
Museum of Fine Arts, 1988.

BOOKS AND CATALOGUES

Bay Area Biennial. Newport Beach, Ca.: Newport
Harbor Art Museum, 1986.

Caiger-Smith, Martin. *Site Work: Architecture in
Photography Since Early Modernism.* London:
Photographers' Gallery, 1991.

Contemporary California Photography. San Francisco:
Camerawork Gallery, 1978.

Janis, Eugenia Parry. *To Collect the Art of Women:
The Jane Reese Williams Collection of Photography.*
Santa Fe: Museum of New Mexico, 1992.

*Large Spaces in Small Places: A Survey of Western
Landscape Photography 1850-1980.* Sacramento:
Crocker Art Museum, 1980.

New American Photography. Tokyo: Min Gallery,
1986.

Roth, Moira, editor. *Connecting Conversations,
Interviews with 28 Bay Area Women Artists.*
San Francisco: Eucalyptus Press, 1989.

*Slices of Time: California Landscapes 1860-1880,
1960-1980.* Oakland: The Oakland Museum, 1985.

Stofflet, Mary. *California Cityscapes.* San Diego:
San Diego Museum of Art, 1992.

Sullivan, Constance. *Women Photographers.* New
York: Harry Abrams, 1990.

SELECTED ARTICLES AND REVIEWS

1977

Fischer, Hal. "The Contemporary Landscape."
Artweek 8, no. 8 (February 19, 1977): 11-12.

—. "Approaches to Landscape: San Francisco Bay
Area." *La Mamelle Magazine: Arts Contemporary* 2,
no. 4 (1977): 18.

Richards, Paul. "American Aesthetic in Plain and
Spooky Places." *Washington Post,* June 18, 1977.

1978

Albright, Thomas. "Photographers with Compelling
Vision. Review: Irving Penn, Marion Post
Wolcott, Catherine Wagner." *San Francisco
Chronicle,* May 6, 1978.

Fischer, Hal. "Contemporary California Landscape:
The West is . . . well, different?" *Afterimage* 6,
no. 4 (November 1978): 4-6.

—. "San Francisco. Catherine Wagner, Simon
Lowinsky Gallery." *Artforum* 18, no.1 (September
1978): 88-89.

Welpott, Jack. "East is East and West is West."
Untitled (Friends of Photography) 14 (1978):
10-13.

1982

Fischer, Hal. "San Francisco. 'Slices of Time:
California Landscapes 1860-1880, 1960-1980,'
The Oakland Museum." *Artforum* 21, no. 2
(October 1982): 77.

Glowen, Ron. "Urban Documentaries." *Artweek* 13,
no. 5 (October 23, 1982): 11.

Thomas, James W. "What Is Not Art?" *Northwest
Photography* (October 1982).

1983

Welpott, Jack. "George Moscone Site."
Picture Magazine 20 (1983): 66-69.

1985

Bloom, John. "Catherine Wagner at the Oakland
Museum." *Photo Metro* 3, no. 28 (April 1985): 14.

Fischer, Hal. "Oakland. Catherine Wagner." *Artforum* 24, no. 2 (October 1985): 129-30.

Murray, Joan. "Studying the Classroom." *Artweek* 16, no. 4 (March 16, 1985): 11.

1986

Baker, Kenneth. "A Bay Area Biennial." *San Francisco Chronicle,* November 9, 1986.

Wilson, William. "The Bay Is on View." *Los Angeles Times,* October 26, 1986.

1987

Muchnic, Suzanne. "American Photography as Seen from Japan." *Los Angeles Times Book Review,* December 20, 1987.

Murray, Joan. "Photography: Books from Exhibitions." *Artweek* 18, no. 42 (December 12, 1987): 15-16.

1988

Chadwick, Susan. "Photo Exhibition Goes to School on the Lessons." *Houston Post,* September 18, 1988.

Grundberg, Andy. "Photography." *New York Times Book Review,* December 4, 1988.

"Holiday Books." *Philadelphia Inquirer,* December 11, 1988.

Reeve, Catherine. "Two Exhibits Coax the Eye to Comprehend as Well as to See." *Chicago Tribune,* October 28, 1988.

1989

Berkson, Bill. "Catherine Wagner, Fraenkel Gallery." *Artforum* 28, no. 3 (November 1989): 160.

Bonetti, David. "A Classification of Classrooms." *San Francisco Examiner,* December 8, 1989.

McCauley, Anne. "Catherine Wagner and Photographs of Urban Change." *Afterimage* 16, no. 6 (January 1989): 14-17.

Ross, Jeanette. "Organizing Meaning." *Artweek* 20, no. 43 (December 21, 1989): 10.

1990

Glowen, Ron. "The Eloquence of Empty Rooms." *Artweek* 21, no. 42 (December 13, 1990): 14.

"Photography." *The New Yorker* 66, no. 8 (April 16, 1990): 19.

Coleman, A.D. "Photography." *The New York Observer,* March 26, 1990.

Levy, Ellen K. "Natural History Re-Created." *Center for Photography at Woodstock Quarterly* 11, no. 4 (1990): 4-11.

1991

Chattopadhyay, Colette. "A Passionate Objectivity." *Artweek* 22, no. 42 (December 12, 1991):1,12.

Fischer, Hal. "A Conversation with Catherine Wagner." *Artweek* 22, no. 42 (December 12, 1991):12-13.

1992

Clifton, Leigh Ann"'. . . the boundaries of strict photographic concern are no longer at issue . . .': A dialogue between Lewis Baltz, Andy Grundberg, Sandra Phillips, and Catherine Wagner." *Artweek* 23, no. 20 (July 23, 1992): 16-21.

CHECKLIST OF THE EXHIBITION

1. *James, Karyl Ann, Patrick, Annelies, Allison, and Robert G., San Francisco, Ca.,* 1989, three gelatin silver prints, 16x60 in.
2. *Coester T., Berkeley, Ca.,* 1990, three gelatin silver prints, 16x60 in.
3. *Erna K., Brookline, Ma.,* 1991, three gelatin silver prints, 16x60 in.
4. *Bert S., Houston, Tx.,* 1991, three gelatin silver prints, 16x60 in.
5. *Michael B. and Ron S., San Francisco, Ca.,* 1992, three gelatin silver prints, 16x60 in.
6. *Ron S. and Peter A., San Francisco, Ca.,* 1989, three gelatin silver prints, 16x60 in.
7. *Irene, Peter, and Josh P., Brookline, Ma.,* 1991, three gelatin silver prints, 16x60 in.
8. *Alexandra M., Houston, Tx.,* 1991, three gelatin silver prints, 16x60 in.
9. *Helen, Robert, Clare, and Chloe R., Newton, Ma.,* 1991, three gelatin silver prints, 16x60 in.
10. *Jean C., San Anselmo, Ca.,* 1991, three gelatin silver prints, 16x60 in.
11. *Sarah F., Kansas City, Mo.,* 1991, three gelatin silver prints, 16x60 in.
12. *Louellen, Darryl, Allison, Darryl, Jr., Brandon, and Ryan B., New Orleans, La.,* 1991, three gelatin silver prints, 16x60 in.
13. *Pat M., Oakland, Ca.,* 1991, three gelatin silver prints, 16x60 in.
14. *Christine T., San Francisco, Ca.,* 1990, three gelatin silver prints, 16x60 in.
15. *Fidel, Graciela, Yesenia, Guillermo, Adrian, and Fidel, Jr., G., Pittsburg, Ca.,* 1992, three gelatin silver prints, 16x60 in.
16. *Marilyn and Bill M., San Lorenzo, Ca.,* 1990, three gelatin silver prints, 16x60 in.
17. *Mimi and Mel K., Brookline, Ma.,* 1991, three gelatin silver prints, 16x60 in.
18. *Maggie N., New Orleans, La.,* 1991, three gelatin silver prints, 16x60 in.
19. *Harold and Margaret R., New Orleans, La.,* 1991, three gelatin silver prints, 16x60 in.
20. *David W. and Annetta F., Richmond, Ca.,* 1990, three gelatin silver prints, 16x60 in.
21. *Val N., San Bruno, Ca.,* 1992, three gelatin silver prints, 16x60 in.
22. *Diane and David G., Piedmont, Ca.,* 1990, three gelatin silver prints, 16x60 in.
23. *Martha, Antonio, Antonio, Jr., and Luis P., Pittsburg, Ca.,* 1992, three gelatin silver prints, 16x60 in.
24. *Johnnie M., San Francisco, Ca.,* 1989, three gelatin silver prints, 16x60 in.
25. *Tom and Pat B., New Orleans, La.,* 1991, three gelatin silver prints, 16x60 in.
26. *William F., Kansas City, Mo.,* 1991, three gelatin silver prints, 16x60 in.
27. *Anne T. and Joe W., Houston, Tx.,* 1991, three gelatin silver prints, 16x60 in.
28. *Monica and Jack P., Mill Valley, Ca.,* 1990, three gelatin silver prints, 16x60 in.
29. *Ann and Robert W., Terra Linda, Ca.,* 1991, three gelatin silver prints, 20x56 in.
30. *Audrey, Jack, Joshua, and Jessica K., Newton Center, Ma.,* 1991, three gelatin silver prints, 16x60 in.
31. *Rose and Parker T., San Francisco, Ca.,* 1989, three gelatin silver prints, 16x60 in.
32. *Gail and Bill K., Alameda, Ca.,* 1991, three gelatin silver prints, 16x60 in.
33. *Barbara M. Albany, Ca.,* 1990, three gelatin silver prints, 16x60 in.
34. *Leonard and Marjorie V., Los Angeles, Ca.,* 1991, three gelatin silver prints, 16x60 in.